GREATER EXPECTATIONS

FRAMES
BARNA GROUP

GREATER EXPECTATIONS

Succeed (and Stay Sane) in an On-Demand,
All-Access, Always-On Age

CLAIRE DIAZ-ORTIZ
RE/FRAME BY DIANE PADDISON

ZONDERVAN®

ZONDERVAN

Greater Expectations
Copyright © 2013 by Barna Group

This title is also available as a Zondervan ebook.
Visit www.zondervan.com/ebooks.

This title is also available in a Zondervan audio edition.
Visit www.zondervan.fm.

Requests for information should be addressed to:

Zondervan, Grand Rapids, Michigan 49530

ISBN 978-0-310-43336-1 (softcover)

Published in association with the literary agency of The Fedd Agency, Inc,
401 Ranch Road 620 South, Suite 350c, Austin, TX 78734.

Cover design and interior graphics: Amy Duty
Interior design: Kate Mulvaney

Printed in the United States of America

13 14 15 16 17 18 /DCI/ 18 17 16 15 14 13 12 11 10 9 8 7 6 5 4 3 2 1

CONTENTS

WHY YOU NEED FRAMES

These days, you probably find yourself with less time than ever.

Everything seems like it's moving at a faster pace—except your ability to keep up.

Somehow, you are weighed down with more obligations than you have ever had before.

Life feels more complicated. More complex.

If you're like most people, you probably have lots of questions about how to live a life that matters. You feel as though you have more to learn than can possibly be learned. But with smaller chunks of time and more sources of information than ever before, where can you turn for real insight and livable wisdom?

Barna Group has produced this series to examine the complicated issues of life and to help you live more meaningfully. We call it FRAMES—like a good set of eyeglasses that help you see the world more clearly ... or a work of art perfectly hung that invites you to look more closely ... or a building's skeleton, the part that is most essential to its structure.

The FRAMES Season 1 collection provides thoughtful and concise, data-driven and visually appealing insights for anyone who wants a more faith-driven and fulfilling life. In each FRAME we couple new cultural analysis from our team at Barna with an essay from leading voices in the field, providing information and ideas for you to digest in a more easily consumed number of words.

After all, it's a fast-paced world, full of words and images vying for your attention. Most of us have a number of half-read or "read someday" books on our shelves. But each FRAME aims to give you the essential information and real-life application behind one of today's most crucial trends in less than one-quarter the length of most books. These are big ideas in small books — designed so you truly can read less but know more. And the infographics and ideas in this FRAME are intended for share-ability. So read it, then find someone to "frame" with these ideas, and keep the conversation going (see "Share This Frame" on page 81).

Furthermore, each FRAME brings a distinctly Christian point of view to today's trends. In times of uncertainty, people look for guides. And we believe the Christian community is trying to make sense of the dramatic social changes happening around us.

Over the past thirty years, Barna Group has built a reputation as a trusted analyst of religion and culture. We offer cultural discernment for the Christian community by thoughtful analysts who care enough to tell the truth about what's really happening in today's society.

So sit back, but not for long. With FRAMES we invite you to read less and know more.

DAVID KINNAMAN
FRAMES, executive producer
president / Barna Group

ROXANNE STONE
FRAMES, general editor
vice president / Barna Group

Learn more at www.barnaframes.com.

FRAMES

TITLE	20 and Something	Becoming Home	Fighting for Peace	Greater Expectations
PURPOSE	Have the Time of Your Life (And Figure It All Out Too)	Adoption, Foster Care, and Mentoring – Living Out God's Heart for Orphans	Your Role in a Culture Too Comfortable with Violence	Succeed (and Stay Sane) in an On-Demand, All-Access, Always-On Age
AUTHOR	David H. Kim	Jedd Medefind	Carol Howard Merritt & Tyler Wigg-Stevenson	Claire Diaz-Ortiz
KEY TREND	27% of young adults have clear goals for the next 5 years	62% of Americans believe Christians have a responsibility to adopt	47% of adults say they're less comfortable with violence than 10 years ago	42% of people are unhappy with their work/life balance

PERFECT FOR SMALL GROUP DISCUSSION

FRAMES Season 1: DVD
FRAMES Season 1: The Complete Collection

READ LESS.
KNOW MORE.

The Hyperlinked Life	Multi-Careering	Sacred Roots	Schools in Crisis	Wonder Women
Live with Wisdom in an Age of Information Overload	Do Work that Matters at Every Stage of Your Journey	Why Church Still Matters	They Need Your Help (Whether You Have Kids or Not)	Navigating the Challenges of Motherhood, Career, and Identity
Jun Young & David Kinnaman	Bob Goff	Jon Tyson	Nicole Baker Fulgham	Kate Harris
71% of adults admit they're overwhelmed by information	75% of adults are looking for ways to live a more meaningful life	51% of people don't think it's important to attend church	46% of Americans say public schools are worse than 5 years ago	72% of women say they're stressed

#BarnaFrames

www.barnaframes.com

BEFORE YOU READ

....

- Did you check your phone for messages while you were still in bed this morning? Did you check it right before going to bed last night? If so, what do you think has shaped your current phone habits?

- When was the last time you intentionally took a break—several hours, a day, or more—from online activity? How did you feel during and after that time away?

- When you take a break at work, have to wait in line somewhere, or sit in a waiting room for an appointment, how likely are you to use that time to engage on social media?

- How have you noticed your level of connectedness— especially if you are "always on"—hindering your productivity rather than helping it?

- What "off-line" activities do you most enjoy? How do you intentionally make time for them?

- What are some words you would use to describe the pace of your life right now? Are you satisfied with that pace or hoping to change it?

- What types of activities—scheduling, intentional breaks, exercise, list-making—do you find help you to be the most productive and effective?

barnaframes.com

GREATER EXPECTATIONS

Succeed (and Stay Sane) in an On-Demand,
All-Access, Always-On Age

INFOGRAPHICS

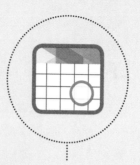

Living in an age of
GREATER EXPECTATIONS

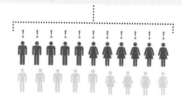

UNSATISFIED...

When we're stressed out, there isn't a lot of room
for satisfaction. In fact, less than half of adults profess
to feeling satisfied in any of the following areas:

42%

*Work/life
balance*

39%

*Overall
rest*

38%

*Relationship
boundaries*

28%

*Overall
stress levels*

AND STRESSED OUT

More than half of adults felt physically or mentally overwhelmed at least once last month. An alarming one-fifth of adults say they felt that way five times or more. This number is particularly high among Millennials and women.

"Last month, I felt physically or mentally overwhelmed ..."

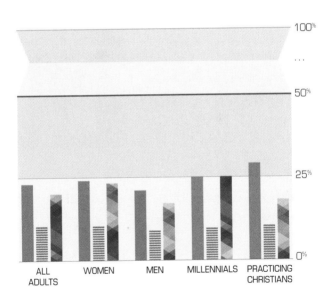

100%

...

50%

25%

0%

ALL ADULTS   WOMEN   MEN   MILLENNIALS   PRACTICING CHRISTIANS

1– 2 times   *3 – 4 times*   *5+ times*

A (very) LITTLE R&R

The demands on our time and energy are pretty relentless these days, and we aren't finding a lot of time for rest. Even when we do, our ideas of "rest" still include a lot of work.

● I SET ASIDE...

1 / Time each day to spend with God: 21%

2 / Time each day to spend alone: 16%

3 / One day a week for rest: 14%

4 / Time each day for an activity that recharges me: 12%

5 / A time each day when I don't use electronics: 12%

WHAT DO YOU DO ON YOUR DAY OF REST?

44%

Enjoyable work

37%

Non-enjoyable work if it needs to be done

19%

No work at all

A ROUTINE FOR REST

When looking for a boost of energy to recharge,
adults engage in these go-to activities:

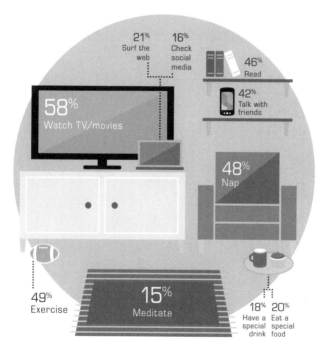

21% Surf the web

16% Check social media

46% Read

42% Talk with friends

58% Watch TV/movies

48% Nap

49% Exercise

15% Meditate

18% Have a special drink

20% Eat a special food

GREATER EXPECTATIONS

Succeed (and Stay Sane) in an On-Demand,
All-Access, Always-On Age

FRAMEWORK

BY BARNA GROUP

Here are some facts about life in an age of greater expectations:

- More people have access to smartphones than toilets.[1]

- Three million new blogs come online every month.[2]

- The top 100 cat videos generate 1 million views per day on YouTube—*just* cat videos.

- Psychiatrists are beginning to identify Internet overuse as a psychological disorder.[3]

If you ever check your smartphone before getting out of bed, log on to email on vacation, compare yourself to friends on Instagram, compulsively update your Twitter feed, or get overwhelmed with every buzz and beep of your digital armory—this book is for you.

In our FRAMES survey, we asked people like you about their social media use and their sense of burnout. Here's what we found.

The Social Americans

Today, a one-year-old may be able to intuit the use of an iPad Touch, but not even five years ago this was unthinkable. As our technology changes, so do we. Over the last thirty years, digital media have transformed the way people in the US live, work, and interact with one another.

Common experience already tells us most of our friends

and family members are active on at least one social media site. By far, the most popular is Facebook — almost two-thirds of adults (63%) are on "The Social Network." Among Facebook users, more than half (58%) say they use it daily and more than four out of five (85%) use it at least once a week.

Other social media sites — LinkedIn (23% of adults), Pinterest (20%), Twitter (17%), and Instagram (14%) — lag behind Facebook in number of users and frequency of use. Though Instagram, now owned by Facebook, has the next highest engagement with 42% daily users, the vast majority of people on social media (84%) still consider Facebook to be their primary social media network.

Americans' connectivity doesn't stop with social media, however. Almost two-thirds of adults say they are online one to five hours a day and one in ten say they are online five to more than twelve hours daily. The numbers are even more striking among younger generations. Nearly one-quarter of adults aged eighteen to twenty-nine are online five hours or more per day, and most young adults (83%) are connected at least one hour a day, compared to 75% among the general population. The FRAMES data also show women use social media more than men. Pinterest is the most lopsided social network — for every man who logs in, three women do likewise.

Practicing Christians are on par with the average American when it comes to social media use and online presence, but they display some distinguishable practices. More than one-quarter of US adults (28%)

utilize the Internet for some aspect of their faith experience. That number jumps to more than half of all practicing Christians (54%), with one-quarter of the aforementioned (24%) using the Internet as part of their religious devotion on at least a weekly basis, if not daily (8%).

The most common online faith-based activity is reading a challenging or inspirational message; over half of Christians say this is their primary activity. Other faith-related activity includes listening to religious teachings via social media (43%), buying spiritual books online (34%), or submitting prayer requests digitally (28%).

However, this is where digitally plugged-in Christians are faced with a quandary: Is the endless wealth of online spiritual resources only adding to the digital deluge, contributing in some way to the feelings of being crazy busy and overwhelmed? How can Christians make the most of the resources for spiritual and personal growth at their fingertips while maintaining a healthy balance of media consumption?

The New Working Class

From email to sharable online documents, our digital and often mobile devices allow us to be more connected and more able to work anytime and anywhere. Yet American adults are split on whether or not their digital devices actually do make them more productive (47%) or if they've become a distraction to productivity (53%). In a typical day, only a third of Americans say they spend five to eight hours on real, productive work. Another quarter say they only get about three to five hours of productive work time, and about one in five (19%) say they spend eight to twelve hours being productive. So, while most Americans (74%) still feel their days are truly productive, a majority (55%) admit to wishing they'd accomplished more the day before. It would seem that no matter how much we get done, these days it's never enough. The expectations are high and getting higher.

So how are Americans managing the ever-increasing demands of a digital age? Nearly four out of five people (78%) create lists. About a quarter of people (23%) schedule specific tasks for the time of day when they're most productive—something a little more than half of people (54%) say they know about themselves. But, even with their lists in place, Americans are not happy with the level of stress in their lives, and many admit to being on the verge of burnout.

When Digital Lights Burn Out

The truth is "digital overwhelm" isn't news to any of us. Most Americans already know they're taking on too much and running the risk of burnout. More than half of respondents (53%) say they felt physically or mentally overwhelmed by their digital life at least once in the previous month. Generally, women (57%) are more likely to feel digitally overwhelmed than men (47%). This gender gap is even wider among Protestants. In this faith segment, two-thirds of women feel overwhelmed by this constant flow of media compared to just over half of practicing Christian men (54%). Yet both Christian men and women alike are more overwhelmed than the national average.

The stress experienced by the sheer volume of digital distraction may be spilling into other arenas of life as well. Less than half of Americans (42%) feel satisfied with the ever-tenuous work/life balance, and even fewer are content with relationship boundaries (38%), overall stress (28%), and their practice of rest (39%).

Many commentators suggest Americans' constant connectivity is linked with an inability across the nation to practice rest and relaxation. At the very least, such analysts are right about one thing: American adults are not particularly good at rest. Only a little over half of Americans (54%) say they relax on a regular basis—leaving nearly half who do not. Even fewer find space in their schedules to exercise (45%), enjoy a hobby (44%), spend time with friends (42%), or pray or meditate (37%). Americans are so stressed, in fact, that when asked to rank a list of life objectives, the top desire adults expressed is a good night's rest.[4] This inability to rest is perhaps a side effect of an inability to set boundaries. Four in ten Americans admit they cannot say "no" to additional activities.

While Christians generally mirror the national practice —or lack thereof—of rest, there is one notable exception: two-thirds of practicing Christians find time for prayer and meditation compared to just one-third of the general population. Practicing Protestant women, in particular, make time for this discipline—three-

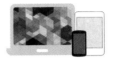

quarters say they make a regular practice of prayer compared to nearly two-thirds of practicing Protestant men.

Emotional boundaries are often even harder to gauge, and one area many people struggle with online is envy. Although adults typically think they are above average when compared to others (what psychologists refer to as "illusory superiority"), this effect is largely absent when it comes to social media. Online users have a generally high view of those they interact with online, saying when compared to their own life, online friends seem more successful (22%), creative (21%), wealthy (18%), respected (14%), attractive (13%), disciplined (11%), and content (10%) than they personally are. Even though these percentages may seem relatively low,

Friends online seem more ...

22% *Successful* than me

21% *Creative* than me

18% *Wealthy* than me

14% *Respected* than me

13% *Attractive* than me

10% *Content* than me

they tell us many users of social media are making value judgments about others as they spend time online.

Being exposed to the best sides of our peers and colleagues has a downside: Comparing ourselves with others often results in a lower self-perception. In fact, more than one-quarter of social media users (27%) say social media use makes them feel worse about themselves.

Taking a Break from Burnout

It's not surprising, then, that many of us express a desire to take some sort of a break from the digital matrix. Still, it's uncommon to set aside a Sabbath of sorts from social media use. A majority of Americans (60%) say they've never taken an intentional break from social media. Only 17% of Americans have quit a social media permanently, and about one in five (21%) have taken a break from one network for awhile. Practicing Christians are essentially the same when it comes to their digital practices on this front: a majority never take intentional breaks from their devices.

When people do take a break from digital demands, what do they do? They might exercise (49%), nap (48%), or read (46%). The majority of adults (58%) feel taking care of household chores or phoning a friend or family member are acceptable restful activities.

Yet ideas of what constitutes a Sabbath differ drastically among Americans. Significantly, 43% view the use of smartphones, tablets, computers, and TV as suitable for

WHAT DO YOU DO ON YOUR DAY OF REST?

44%	37%	19%
Enjoyable work	*Non-enjoyable work if it needs to be done*	*No work at all*

a day of rest. In fact, the national majority (58%) uses their "alone time" to watch TV or a movie and consider it part of their daily recharge routine. In contrast, only 15% of Americans say they meditate to reenergize.

Unquestionably, the digital age has changed the way we live, work, and relate to one another. Caught in the wake of ever-expanding digital technologies that often demand more and more from us, Americans still feel productive—but they also feel overwhelmed, stressed, and burned out with the pace of digitalized American life. Many idealize the concept of logging off periodically, if only for a little while, but few actually do so.

This FRAME is meant to help—to get a grip on the things that seem to be spinning out of control and to not only stay sane but succeed in a time of greater and greater expectations. Claire Diaz-Ortiz, an early employee at Twitter, is a digital pioneer in her own right. Referred to as "The Woman Who Got the Pope on Twitter,"[5] Claire leads Twitter's social good initiatives and is the author of *Twitter for Good: Change the World One Tweet at a Time.* As someone who makes her living online, she has also learned—through trial and error—how to make a life off-line. In this FRAME, she shares some of her hard-learned lessons for making a rich and rewarding life and career in the midst of myriad digital demands.

We may know how to sync our digital devices across platforms, multiply our Twitter followers, or text in our sleep, but this widespread sense of burnout tells us we still have much to learn. These are the paradoxes—overwhelmed, yet productive; over-committed, yet highly connected; burned out, but still going—that need to be addressed to navigate the greater expectations we feel in the digital age. ◆

GREATER EXPECTATIONS

Succeed (and Stay Sane) in an On-Demand,
All-Access, Always-On Age

THE FRAME

BY CLAIRE DIAZ-ORTIZ

The alarm goes off.

You roll over and hit snooze.

Seven minutes later, the alarm goes off again.

You let the radio play this time, and the day's early news seeps into your consciousness, waking you up to what you missed while you were sleeping. Murder. War. Expert analysis on Brad Pitt's new facial hair. You reach for your smartphone to help you get your bearings. Ignoring the pink-gold magic of morning light, you swipe the screen, craving that first hit of gambler's rush—"There might be something exciting in my in-box!"—as much or more than your first caffeine fix.

You lie in bed for the next ten minutes, not even hearing the drone of radio news as you scroll through emails, texts, tweets, and Facebook updates. "I'm just doing triage before the day begins," you tell yourself, making sure no disaster has unfolded since you checked your phone seconds before falling asleep six hours ago.

Finally you drag yourself out of bed and, after showering, caffeinating, and possibly commuting, you're at your desk. Before you begin work for the day, you log on for your next digital fix, this time starting at a big hi-def screen. Over the next hour, you reread emails you saw ninety minutes ago but put off dealing with until later, read new messages that have been delivered since early this morning, delete newsletters you don't have time to unsubscribe from, and generally try to make your in-box feel a bit less daunting. You think, "Oh, look. Sarah, Dylan, Mark, and crazy Aunt Judy all sent links that look pretty interesting," and before you know it, you've consumed enough information to start your own online news syndicate, where celebrity baby names get equal billing with international financial crises. Consume, consume, consume.

Sixty minutes later, you (1) have eighteen tabs open on your browser, (2) just bought a book from Amazon recommended by a Facebook friend you've never met in real life, and (3) click over to TMZ to see if there's any new info on Brad Pitt's beard. That's when you (4) realize your coffee cup is, for the second time since you arrived at work, empty and (5) you have accomplished absolutely nothing, and you're already burned out.

Time for that third cup of coffee.

The Overwhelm Epidemic

Sound familiar? You are not alone. In the month before taking our FRAMES survey, more than half of respondents (53%) felt physically or mentally overwhelmed at least once by their digital lives. One in five (20%) felt overwhelmed *five or more times* in a single month. We are in the midst of an epidemic of "overwhelm."

Human beings have always had to cope with seasons of intense stress—political upheavals, major life changes, family tragedies, daily dramas, and even positive, planned events, such as weddings and births. Throughout history, our bodies' stress reactions have

Who has time FOR STRESS?

Our always-on lifestyle is taking its toll. More than half of adults admit to feeling physically or mentally overwhelmed at least once in the last month and an overwhelming one in five hit the end of their rope at least five times in the last 30 days.

10%	3–4 times a month
20%	5+ times a month
23%	1–2 times a month

53%
felt physically or mentally overwhelmed at least once last month

helped us respond wisely to short periods of acute pressure. But in the last two decades, brief episodes of stress have become longer and more frequent (and more damaging), aggravated by our on-demand, all-access digital reality. Our natural fight-or-flight response, perfectly engineered to help us survive occasional, immediate danger, is now our default setting. We refresh our in-boxes and Twitter feeds every five minutes, desperately seeking that hit of adrenaline to course through our strung-out, junkie veins: "Someone retweeted me!" "Marcie had twins!" "Brad Pitt shaved!" The chance a pellet will come down the chute is one in a thousand, but we keep hitting the button like trained lab mice.

When we're always connected, we allow

others—colleagues and celebrities, close friends and distant acquaintances, bloggers and news aggregators—to set our life's agenda. Our ability to prioritize is paralyzed by the sheer volume of requests, demands, opportunities, and information. As a result, productivity or creativity (or both) suffer, and work casts a longer, darker shadow over the rest of our lives. A minority of us (42%) claim satisfaction with work/life balance. And even fewer of us say we're satisfied with the level of stress in our lives (28%) or the amount of rest we're getting (39%).

In *Finding Rest When the Work Is Never Done*, Patrick Klingaman recalls the predictions his generation heard as youngsters that, by the turn of the twenty-first century, the digitization of the American workforce would create a leisure class who worked just twenty to thirty hours a week.[6] Futurists worried and wondered: What would people do with their time? How would the American character change as a result? As we all know, this reality did not materialize. Constant connection, it turns out, means Americans never stop working.

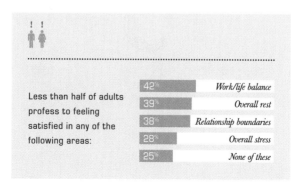

Less than half of adults profess to feeling satisfied in any of the following areas:

42%	Work/life balance
39%	Overall rest
38%	Relationship boundaries
28%	Overall stress
25%	None of these

PRODUCTIVE OR DISTRACTED?

Life might be coming at us fast and furious, but many people report they are actually getting less done. And even when they do feel productive, they don't feel productive *enough*.

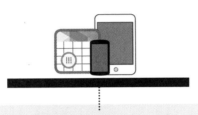

Smart phones and tablets have ...

53%
Become a distraction

47%
Made me more productive

Were you truly productive yesterday?

74%
Yes

26%
No

Do you wish you could have accomplished more yesterday?

55%
Yes

45%
No

Although many of us are aware of activities that would help us bring greater balance to our lives, such as regular rest and exercise, too few of us make these actions a daily priority. Instead, we check our smartphones several times an hour—one study shows an average of thirty-four times a day.[7] But we also entertain growing worries that this handheld wonder-device is distracting us from real productivity rather than making us more effective and efficient.

Productivity enhancers or ever-present distractions—either way, our technology is changing our routines. And our lives are thrown further out of whack every time we choose an empty information fix over life-giving activities such as exercise, reflection, and meditation as well as quality face-to-face time with loved ones. The results are bad for all—and disastrous for some because the harmful consequences of life imbalance are becoming more common and more extreme. A full 12% of us report having experienced a severe mental or physical collapse due to overwork or stress. And given that just 16% of us point to physical illness as the primary cause of our distress, we must at least consider the possibility that our unrelenting connectedness, our habitual "mainlining" of data, has led to a viral outbreak of overwhelm that has infected our minds and hearts.

This isn't the life you and I were meant to live.

You feel it in your bones during those fleeting, quiet moments when you're alone with your thoughts. You confirmed it on vacation last year when you left your smartphone, tablet, and laptop at home and felt the tension in your neck and gut melt away for the first time in months (or years). But you're not sure how to make lasting changes to your habits and lifestyle that will bring the sustainable existence you long for. You have a *job*, after all. You have a *life*, full of family, friends, and colleagues who don't think twice about communicating with you at all hours of the day or night through the very devices that are driving you to distraction.

What can you do? How can you reap the best of technology's blessings without suffering the worst of its curses? Is it even possible to find peace, rest, and that ever-elusive balance in a world of greater and greater expectations?

Understanding the unique pressures of life on the information superhighway is like suddenly becoming aware you're headed the wrong way on the interstate: Until you find an exit ramp, knowing doesn't do you much good. To leave crazy behind and start the journey toward sanity, exit now. Slowly back away from the

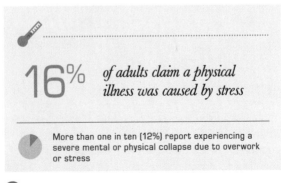

16% *of adults claim a physical illness was caused by stress*

More than one in ten (12%) report experiencing a severe mental or physical collapse due to overwork or stress

phone (as in, leave it silenced in the next room just for an hour) and read on. You can do it!

The PRESENT Principle

The first, and by far the most important, step you can take toward a sustainable and successful life — enhanced instead of dominated by digital tools — is to begin every day by creating a buffer of mental, physical, and spiritual well-being. Mornings set the course of your day. Even in stressful seasons, you can increase your ability to cope well by using your morning routine to build up reserves of peace and mental clarity that will see you through the craziest of circumstances.

Whether you're an early or late riser, setting aside quiet time first thing will put you in the driver's seat of your day. The truth is, you have more control than you might think. Sure, you can't control each and every event that rears its head — but you, and only you, are in control of your responses to those events. Self-control is easiest to exert in the morning, before the day's demands wear down your defenses. In *Willpower: Rediscovering the Greatest Human Strength*, renowned psychologist Roy F. Baumeister argues that willpower, like a muscle, becomes fatigued with overexertion.[8] So before your willpower gets a cramp, direct it early in the day toward healthy, life-giving activities that help you cultivate a reserve of sanity. By growing your margin of peace early on, you'll end the day with well-being to spare.

By leading your morning, you lead your life.

My days used to get away from me. Between morning iPhone pillow time and nightly iPhone pillow time, I zigzagged through my days without rhyme or reason, plugging important and not-so-important activities into random time slots until my fifteen (or sixteen or eighteen) hours of waking life were spent. It was ineffective and exhausting, and I was a mess. I needed to make some changes—pronto.

I'm a fan of acronyms. They help me organize my thoughts and intentions and make it more likely I'll actually do what I've decided in advance is important. I have used what I now call the PRESENT Principle for years, but it wasn't always called that. For a while, it was a nonsensical string of consonants that reminded me of the seven actions I wanted to take every day to help me live in healthy balance. I used to write this string of hard-to-remember letters on scraps of paper to keep my action steps in the forefront of my mind throughout the day, until my desk, car, kitchen counter, and purse were absolutely littered. I finally admitted I needed a more memorable acronym when I handed the pharmacist a

P.R.E.S.E.N.T.

P	R	E	S	E	N	T
Pray*	Read	Express	Schedule	Exercise	Nourish	Track

*or Pause or Peace

prescription from my doctor and she asked, "What's 'JJEMMPR'?"

And that's how the PRESENT Principle was born. Each letter corresponds to a daily action that helps me widen my margin of mental, spiritual, and physical well-being. Together, the first four steps constitute my morning practice, while I usually do the last three later in the day.

P = Pray (or Pause or Peace)

R = Read

E = Express

S = Schedule

E = Exercise

N = Nourish

T = Track

When I wake in the mornings, I often remind myself that practicing this routine is a *present*. Each day, I give myself a gift by setting aside time and attention to cultivate my soul. The PRESENT Principle is a powerful way to proactively organize, or "visioneer," my day for balance and protect myself from the creeping virus of overwhelm.

Let's look at each of the seven steps and how to incorporate them into a daily practice. While the particulars of each of these steps may not all work for you, consider how the *principles* behind them might contribute to your well-being, and ask yourself how you can incorporate those practices and postures in a way that makes the most sense for your personality and lifestyle.

Step 1: Pray

We all long for peace, but there is no way to get it without making time for it. By deliberately pausing to get in touch with our own thoughts and with God through prayer, we create the conditions necessary for peace.

Prayer. Meditation. Silence. Contemplation. These practices draw our thoughts away from the minutia of daily details that so easily distracts us from a greater reality. The poet who wrote Psalm 29 challenges his reader to "Ascribe to the LORD glory and strength. Ascribe to the LORD the glory due his name; worship the LORD in the splendor of his holiness" (vv. 1–2). He follows that challenge with line after line of vivid language that attempts to describe the indescribable: the beauty, power, and awe-inspiring magnitude of an encounter with the Divine. Then he ends his poem with these lines: "The LORD gives strength to his people; the LORD blesses his people with peace (v. 11).

Isn't it interesting that *peace* is the outcome when we direct our attention beyond ourselves toward Someone or something greater? Whether you *pray*, *pause* to reflect, or simply sit in silence to make space for *peace*, giving yourself the gift of a few quiet moments before you launch into your day can ground you in a reality much, much bigger than your client meeting at ten, the dry cleaning that needs to be dropped off, and the overdue electricity bill. It won't take very many days of practice for these moments to feel absolutely essential.

On most mornings, peace comes for me through prayer. Other days, meditation connects me to God's presence. Sometimes staring out the window at the new day dawning with my hands around a mug of hot tea does the trick. Usually my pause for peace is silent, but occasionally listening to beautiful music is its own special kind of prayer.

The point is, before you do anything work-related or tech-related, make time for peace. Make space for peace. You don't have to do it the same way every day, but do it. Leave your iPhone on "Do Not Disturb" for one more hour. If you're not sure how to get started, here are some suggestions for cultivating a peaceful atmosphere for your time of prayer:

- A solitary space

- A cozy chair or floor-sitting, whichever works best for you

- A comfortable temperature

- A beautiful view, a peaceful picture, or a candle— something to focus your attention

- Music that soothes you or helps you access your deepest feelings

- Incense, candles, or an oil diffuser to fill your space with fragrance

- A bell to signal the moment's beginning or end

Step 2: Read

I still remember the first time I heard someone use the word *read* to mean more than passing one's eyes along the words on a page.

I had recently moved to Kenya and was living in an orphanage where nearly two hundred children always seemed to be preparing for exams. Seriously. *Always.* It seemed like these students were taking tests every other day. Each night in their study hall sessions above my orphanage apartment, budding scholars crammed all the knowledge they could fit into their overtaxed brains.

"Will you help us read for our exam?" a student asked one evening after dinner.

"Help you *read?*" I wasn't sure I'd heard her correctly. I was no stranger to helping young kids learn to read, but these were teens who already knew the ins and outs of Jack and Jane and their adventures.

That's when I learned about the word *read.* In England and in many of its former colonies, like Kenya, the word *read* is used the way Americans use the word *study.* Later, when I attended graduate school in England, I did not *study* for a degree—I *read* for one.

In the second step of the PRESENT Principle, think of *read* not as a time just to scan and comprehend words on paper or on a Kindle or iPad, but as a time to study the words. To reflect on and engage with the ideas the words represent.

I read two hundred books a year, none of them during my PRESENT time. Instead, the "reading" I do after morning prayer is my chance to study a passage of Scripture and reflect on its meaning or interact with a devotional writing to find its application for my life.

When you *read* in this way, you have to throw everything you learned about speed-reading out the window and embrace diving deep. Reading may mean a daily Bible study written by a scholar or minister you respect that helps you understand the context and meaning of the passage you're studying. Or it may mean skipping the guidebook and jumping headfirst into a book of the Bible you'd like to know better. Or it may mean following a reading plan that takes you through the entire Bible in one, two, or three years.

If you're not religious, though, reading is still a very important step in the PRESENT Principle. Choose an inspiring biography or a motivational book that leads you to reflect on your life and choices. Consider a collection of quotes or daily affirmations that can center your time of prayer (or pause, or peace).

It should go without saying, but I'll say it just in case: Do not *read* online. Using an e-reader is fine, but be sure the Internet connection is disabled so you're not tempted to distraction. Focus exclusively on your reading for at least fifteen minutes. The Web will still be there when you're done.

Here is a list of reading material I have loved through the years:

- *Simple Abundance: A Daybook of Comfort and Joy* and *The Simple Abundance Journal of Gratitude*, both by Sarah Ban Breathnach

- *My Utmost for His Highest* by Oswald Chambers

- *One Thousand Gifts: A Dare to Live Fully Right Where You Are* by Ann Voskamp

- The Bible (I like to read from *The Message*, Eugene Peterson's modern-language paraphrase)

Step 3: Express

When you don't take time to let yourself acknowledge and express what's going on inside, all those pent-up feelings will find a way out—and it probably won't be pretty. Expression is what your soul longs for, and it's impossible to create a buffer of sanity for your workday when your spirit is beating down the door to be heard. So open the door when you're quiet and alone, and invite yourself to say whatever's on your mind. Get it all out: your longings, fears, petty jealousies, hurts, uncertainties, and feelings of anger or rage. Putting it down on paper makes it much less likely to show up in a board meeting or parent-teacher conference later this afternoon.

What should you write about? Anything you'd like. As James Pennebaker explains in *Writing to Heal*, keeping a journal is really just expressing anything that lies in your heart.[9] If you've never kept a journal before, the first step is to just write. Write anything and everything on your mind, whether it's a letter to your realtor or a gluten-free grocery list. Then try to be aware of how you're feeling about all the stuff on your mind — and write that down too. The goal, over time, is to be able to identify your true feelings and write them down. For a great book on starting and sustaining the journaling process, check out *Leaving a Trace: On Keeping a Journal* by Alexandra Johnson.

Once you have no problem sharing your feelings on the page (and maybe even look forward to it), consider adding one or all of the following elements to your PRESENT practice of expression:

- What you learned in your reading and your reflections about it, maybe with some ideas for how to apply it to your life or circumstances.

- Your hopes for the day, week, and year (and maybe even your life, if you're seeing the big picture this morning).

- The big, hard stuff on your mind: fears for your future, stresses of the present, struggles you or loved ones are facing, relationship woes, financial worries, and professional anxieties. All of them. Just get them on paper.

- Things you are grateful for. For me, finishing each journal entry with a prayer of thanks or a list of things I am grateful for is one way I exert self-control over my attitude and mind-set going into the rest of my day.

- The places in your life where you feel at the end of your rope. Where are you burning the candle at both ends? Where do you need to take a step back and reevaluate? Where are you feeling the most stress, pain, or worry?

Step 4: Schedule

Schedule is a bad word for many people. Schedules are the dusty, illegible, oversized appointment books kept by the music teacher you hated so she could pencil in *yet another lesson* that kept you miserably indoors on bright, sunny days when you wanted to be riding your bike instead.

Or maybe that's just me.

I'm willing to bet you have some skeletons in your scheduling closet. In spite of that, however, most of us still believe written schedules are the best way to plan for the day; three-quarters of FRAMES respondents say they create a schedule of specific tasks for the day. Similarly, more than three out of four respondents (78%) swear by list-making as the best way to get their tasks done.

I believe schedules should set you free. The best scheduling prioritizes appointments and tasks that are most important to give you confidence they can and will get done. At the same time, great scheduling is flexible enough that you can change it if you need to (because, from time to time, you *will* need to) without any guilt or neurotic anxiety that you're deviating from "the Schedule."

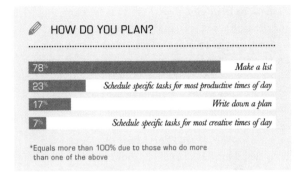

So how can you capture this fabled unicorn?

Throw out every foolproof system and money-back-guaranteed tool and make your own.

First, write it all down. And I do mean all of it — all those nagging thoughts, feelings, and to-dos taking up space in your brain. Writing down recurring thoughts will free "processing power" for you to think other thoughts. So don't keep your mind taxed with remembering things. Write all of your tasks down in a list or as a mind map[10] so you can see everything on your plate at once. (I recommend doing this briefly each day and more in-depth at the start of each week, as I'll explain in more detail later.) Now breathe a sigh of relief, because you don't have to keep reminding yourself to visit the DMV or submit the project proposal for approval. It's on the list. You won't forget.

And now … look at your list. I mean *really* look at it.

Since your brain no longer has to reserve storage space for the DMV, use it to prioritize today's tasks. Pick only a few (one to three) crucial items to complete, along with a handful of less demanding or less time-consuming to-dos. Then slot all the items around the appointments already confirmed in today's schedule, keeping in mind that you may have to switch tasks between available time slots if a meeting goes long or you get stuck in traffic. But even if the unexpected happens, don't freak out. Pick another item from today's list that can be completed more quickly than the task you originally scheduled, and then move on. Remember that big things can be accomplished in small moments. No, really. In *The Clockwork Muse*, a guidebook for writers, Eviatar Zerubavel argues that short pockets of time, used wisely, are more than enough to complete large projects over time.[11]

It may take a few days or even weeks to find the sweet spot between too many and not enough tasks for your daily schedule. And while it might be tempting to try to squeeze a dozen to-dos into your available hours, guard against over scheduling. As Amy Lynn Andrews explains in her wonderful book *Tell Your Time*, you are able to focus better and complete tasks more quickly when you allow yourself a few minutes of downtime between completing one task and starting another.[12]

Remember, a schedule should be a realistic approximation of what you can reasonably accomplish during an actual day of your real life—not an excuse to beat yourself up or run around as if your hair were on fire. The whole point of using your brain's power to prioritize is to spend the day's precious hours doing important things. Superman and Wonder Woman are fantasies, so don't waste your time pretending you can do it all. You can't. But you *can* do the handful of tasks that are most important to you, and you can do them well.

Step 5: Exercise

Morning is not always the best time to do the fifth step of the PRESENT Principle, but it is still crucial for building up your reserves of well-being. Find the time of day that works best for you and your schedule, and set aside time to *exercise*.

Exercise is not my favorite word. But we've all heard a million times how necessary it is not only for physical health but for mental and emotional health as well. So I've tried to change my mind about it because I need all the help I can get. Listening to the Simple Mom podcast (simplemom.net) awhile back, I heard founder Tsh Oxenreider talking with Rachel Meeks, creator of Small Notebook (smallnotebook.org), about the importance of exercise. Rachel said something that has really stuck with me. For her, the key to getting excited about physical fitness was scrapping the word *exercise* from her vocabulary and latching on to the word *move*.[13] This totally clicked for me. Now, rather than setting a goal for my workout — "I'll burn four hundred calories; I'll run for twenty minutes" — I just get moving. The best way for me to finish a twenty-minute run is to start running. When I'm beginning to feel the burn around the nine-minute mark and wondering if I should just stop now, I think, "Nah, I'll just keep moving." And sooner or later, I move myself right across the finish line.

Thinking about exercise this way is, I'm convinced, the reason I've run marathons. It's the reason I've hiked to Everest Base Camp. I am *not* athletic. But I am persistent and—*man!* The high of doing something you thought you never could or going farther than you ever imagined possible is fantastic. And wanting to feel it again is a great motivator to get moving.

Running may not be your cup of tea, and that's perfectly fine. Maybe the camaraderie of team sports or the mental and physical challenge of yoga is more appealing. Just get moving. Find a way to move that you can do and then do it. Don't set intimidating goals that will keep you from getting started, like three-hour bike rides or fifty reps on the bench press. And don't rely on fancy equipment or membership dues to motivate you. The gym industry's bread and butter are the new memberships opened in January and abandoned by March. Don't fall for it.

Not sure where to start? Here are a few ideas to get you moving in the right direction:

- Take a walk through the park with a friend

- Turn up the music and dance with your kids (or by yourself)

- Go for a bike ride

- Plan a day trip to a nearby state park or nature reserve and explore

- Rake the leaves or do other yard work (riding the mower doesn't count)

- Pick up trash around your neighborhood

- Take an exercise class

- Find a video so you can work out in your living room

- Join a church or club's "just for fun" volleyball or softball league

- Teach your kids (or someone else's) how to jump rope double-Dutch

- Volunteer to walk an elderly or ill person's dog

- See how high you can go on a swing (talk about abs of steel!)

Just get moving. Don't think about the finish. Don't worry about beating your time or personal best. Get moving today. And then get moving again tomorrow.

Step 6: Nourish

If so far you feel like the PRESENT Principle is all about discipline and sacrifice, I hope this step will change your mind. *Nourish* is about doing the good things that make you feel great, whether it's plunging your hands into a garden's rich earth, cooking the perfect risotto, or reading a good book curled up on a cozy window seat.

To have a productive day that guards you from burnout, you absolutely must nourish yourself. And remember, *nourishing* means "healthy, nutritious, and life-giving." In *The Happiness Project*, Gretchen Rubin makes the important point that a positive activity does not make you feel guilty for doing it.[14] It's true: You can't nourish yourself with vices. Watching a "reality" dating show or updating your Amazon wish list may be a great way to pass an hour. But let's be honest—they probably don't have much nutritional value for your soul. Nourishing yourself is taking time to invest in an activity that inspires you to be your best and makes you feel fully alive.

Need some ideas for great ways to nourish yourself? Here are a few of my favorites:

- Read a novel

- Browse an architectural or design magazine

- Bake or cook

- Knit

- Paint

- Write

- Wrap a gift

- Play hopscotch

- Pick fruit

- Plant herbs

- Make a smoothie (not for breakfast but just for fun)

- Take a bath

- Listen to beautiful music

- Dance in a room alone

- Sing along to a favorite song

- Play a musical instrument

- Do a crossword or Sudoku puzzle

- Listen to a favorite podcast

Your nourish activities should be brief enough that you can do at least one each day, every day. (The week-long yoga retreat, while wonderful, is not the right fit.) Find small, interesting ways to add joy to your life and feed your creativity and imagination. The nourish step is not just another thing to check off your list, and it should not be combined with a necessary task. For example, whipping up a delicious afternoon smoothie is a great way to take a few minutes for yourself to feed your spirit (and your taste buds), but if you have a smoothie for breakfast on your way out the door, does that count as your nourish time? Nope. Nourishing yourself means

I set aside ...

21%

1 / *Time each day to spend with God*

16%

2 / *Time each day to spend alone*

14%

3 / *One day a week for rest*

12%

4 / *Time each day for an activity that recharges me*

12%

5 / *A time each day when I don't use electronics*

stopping other activities to focus on something that revitalizes and refreshes you. Don't multitask your soul.

Setting aside even as little as fifteen minutes to read for pleasure is one of my favorite activities to nourish my spirit and imagination. I love to read, but I also love knowing at the end of the day that I prioritized doing something good for myself. When you're doing your nourish activity, you may find it necessary to remind yourself you're doing something that's good for you. In fact, that's a great idea: tell yourself you're worth it. Taking time to nourish is as much about experiencing self-care and self-love as it is about the activity itself.

Step 7: Track

In my opinion, "Marcel the Shell with Shoes On" is one of the best YouTube video series of all time. Marcel is a tiny talking seashell who wears very large shoes and shares his thoughts, both mundane and profound (and always random), about life as a half-inch-high shell with oversize footwear. One of the best stories Marcel tells is about his car—which is actually an insect. As Marcel the Shell explains, having a bug for a car is not easy. You may not have to worry about seat belts and automatic door locks, but you've still got your share of problems when it comes to getting somewhere. Bugs are not reliable at reaching a predetermined destination. They just kind of go where they go.

One time maple syrup was spilled on the floor of the kitchen in the house where Marcel lives. Every time Marcel got in his car to go somewhere—to buy groceries or pick up the little Shells from soccer practice, for instance—his car took him instead to the maple syrup spill.[15]

Fun? Maybe.

Productive? No. It might be fun to go with the flow and spend most of the day flying around to maple syrup spills, but it doesn't get you where you want to go. That's why the last step in the PRESENT Principle is so important. When you *track* where you've been and what you've done today, you can see if you got where you wanted to go or if you got distracted by maple syrup.

Tracking your day is not about checking boxes to confirm you completed each of the seven PRESENT Principle steps. The goal, after all, is not to do all the steps for their own sake — heaven knows none of us needs yet another reason to feel guilty. The goal is more sanity, not less! Tracking is about assessing what areas of your life still feel out of whack and then adjusting the PRESENT steps accordingly. Maybe what you're studying when you *read* is putting you to sleep instead of lighting your fire. When you track your day, make a note of it. Then, in tomorrow's *pray* or *express* time, reflect on what to do about it. Will you order a commentary to help you understand what you're reading in the book of Job? Will you change to a Bible study workbook that keeps you more actively engaged? Or will you move your reading time to a spot with better light and fresh air?

Give yourself grace. Reinventing your way of life to thrive in an always-on world can't be done overnight. At the end of the day, when you *track* where you went, what you did, and the PRESENT steps you took (or didn't take), celebrate your successes, however small they may seem. If you *prayed* and *read* before checking your email, bravo! You put some well-being in the bank. Sure, your life will be even more in balance when you can make it through all four of the morning PRESENT steps before hooking yourself up to a data IV, but half an hour is nothing short of a victory. So celebrate it, and then decide what you will do to add interest to your well-being account tomorrow.

Just before bed, review your efforts to include all seven steps at some point during your day. What worked?

What didn't? Take a minute or two to jot down a few notes for your reflection time tomorrow morning—and then sleep soundly, knowing you are cultivating an inner life that can thrive in a digital world.

Remember, this isn't about doing each step just so; it's about finding the practices that work for you. The purpose of building PRESENT time into your day is to prioritize—first thing—the vitality and balance you've been missing. By choosing positive, life-giving activities that bulk up your reserves of peace and clarity, you are protecting yourself from overwhelming digital demands and prioritizing what's most important. A daily routine of stepping away from your devices is key to immunizing yourself against digital burnout and viral overwhelm.

Speaking of Productivity . . .

Cultivation of life-giving habits is one key to warding off burnout, and the other is getting important stuff done. There is a reason people who are *behind* and people who are *burned out* are often the same people. One of the problems with the truckload of information we are called on to manage every day is the superhuman levels of brain power it takes to absorb, filter, process, and curate. And all that time and energy spent on info-digestion is time and energy *not* spent on the projects and tasks that are central to success.

So how do you make the most of your time and brain cells and make technology serve your goals? Here are a few of the ways I channel my resources toward real productivity.

Scan to Plan

To-do lists are personal, and different folks find different variations work best for their profession or temperament. More than three-quarters of people surveyed (78%) keep a to-do list. And when it comes to scheduling those tasks, about a quarter schedule their day with specific tasks and about three-quarters of people work with broad goals instead of specific tasks in mind. I hope to convince both sides to try something I like to call "Scan to Plan."[16] If you're a just-today person, you will like that you come away from your morning scan with a plan for today. If you're a multiple-day person, you will like that you keep a running big-picture list that gives you a snapshot of everything. Regardless of your list-making preference, scanning to plan can boost your productivity by helping you zero in on the to-dos that really matter.

Scanning to plan goes like this: Each morning during your PRESENT time (usually during *schedule*), use a blank sheet of paper to write down everything you need to remember—big tasks and little tasks, items you need from the store, calls you need to make, appointments you need to keep or change. Write down absolutely everything. If it's helpful, think about the key areas of your life—home, relationships, work, kids, church, health, shopping, and so on—and write down what needs to get done in each area. If you've never attempted

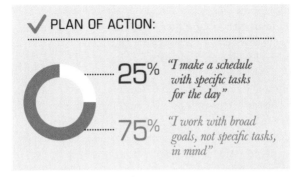

25% *"I make a schedule with specific tasks for the day"*

75% *"I work with broad goals, not specific tasks, in mind"*

something like this, it may feel overwhelming, and that's what you're trying to fix, right? But stick with me. The result for most people who try scanning to plan is the feeling, after just a couple of days, that they have a handle on their always-on lives for the first time in ... maybe forever.

Once your complete scan is on paper, you're ready to plan. Pull out the items you need to accomplish today and make your to-do list. (I suggest you review the earlier section on scheduling to brush up on making the most of your time.) Then pull out the items that need doing later this week and be sure they make an appearance on tomorrow's scan. Finally, tuck the list of remaining non-urgent items in your journal and breathe a sigh of relief. You don't have to keep reminding yourself about those. They're written down. They will get done when it's time to do them, and you don't have to waste another minute thinking about them until then.

Obviously, today's list is made up of what you need to focus on accomplishing today. Don't worry about tomorrow's list or the next day's. You'll make those lists when it's time to make them.

Although it may seem redundant to do a fresh scan of absolutely everything each morning, redundancy is a feature, not a flaw, of scanning to plan. We've already touched on how writing down all the pending reminders and mental notices floating around in the cloud of your mind frees you to focus your brain cells on your priorities. But another big plus of rescanning every morning is the constantly refreshing snapshot of everything in your life that demands your attention. You can't make sound, sane decisions about how to spend your precious time and energy if you only have a vague idea about what needs doing. How can you evaluate whether you have too much on your plate if you can only see the edge of it out of the corner of your eye?

Scanning to plan both gives you a list of what's most important today and gives you essential information about the longer-term sustainability of your lifestyle. It is not a problem to have a lot going on; after all, you're practicing the fine art of prioritization and learning how to make all your time count. But if you are consistently unable to complete your high-priority to-do list, consider whether you need less to do or more help to get it done. Then make it a priority to say no or to delegate.

Try scanning to plan. I think you will find each day's energy channeled toward the things that matter most. And that is a very good definition of productive.

Do Your Biggest Task First, and Do It Off-Line

Most people are most productive first thing in the morning—at least after caffeine. More than 50% of men and women surveyed report being most productive before eleven a.m.

So the first thing we do with our day should be the most important. This is the driving force behind the notion of a morning routine that brings peace and richness to our lives. Unfortunately, though the morning PRESENT steps contribute to our overall well-being, they don't whittle down our to-do lists. So to exploit the magic of mornings for great productivity, make your most important task the first item on your list after your PRESENT time. Don't save it for later. Get it done while the getting is good.

Some people refer to getting the big-ticket to-do out of the way as "eating the frog," thanks to Brian Tracy's best-selling book, *Eat That Frog!* How apt. Just as tucking in to a breakfast of green eggs and frog is probably not high on your list of favorite activities, so the important task on your to-do list is not likely something you're looking forward to. But if the frog must be eaten, it sure makes sense to get it out of the way while you have the willpower to choke it down and get on with your day.[17]

Eating the frog is unpleasant, but you can make it as painless as possible by channeling all your energy and willpower toward completing the task. In plain

How do you
PLAN YOUR DAY?

MOST PRODUCTIVE TIME OF DAY:

More than half of Americans (54%) say they know what time of day they are most productive—and it's generally in the mornings.

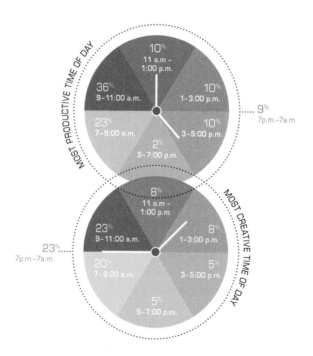

MOST PRODUCTIVE TIME OF DAY

10%
11 a.m – 1:00 p.m.

36%
9–11:00 a.m.

10%
1–3:00 p.m.

23%
7–9:00 a.m.

10%
3–5:00 p.m.

2%
5–7:00 p.m.

9%
7 p.m.–7 a.m.

8%
11 a.m – 1:00 p.m.

23%
9–11:00 a.m.

8%
1–3:00 p.m.

20%
7–9:00 a.m.

5%
3–5:00 p.m.

5%
5–7:00 p.m.

23%
7 p.m.–7 a.m.

MOST CREATIVE TIME OF DAY

MOST CREATIVE TIME OF DAY:

Only about one-fifth of adults (21%) know what time of day they are most creative. For those who do, mid-morning and late at night seem to bring the creative juices.

terms, put your phone in a drawer, close your browser, disable chat or instant messaging, turn off your email notifications, and *focus*. Whether you are designing a PowerPoint or Keynote presentation, drafting a report, practicing a speech, or paying bills, limit your information consumption so you can pay attention to your own thoughts and ideas.

Take Breaks

Whether you are plowing through your most challenging task of the day (let's say, putting together a grant proposal) or working on one of the lesser tasks you have relegated to a time you are less energetic (calling the insurance company, maybe), take regular breaks to keep burnout at bay.

Resist the urge to keep going when you feel hungry, thirsty, or annoyed. Instead, take a five-minute break. Don't check Twitter or Facebook or text with your mom. While a five-minute Facebook check-in might sound like a well-deserved reward after working for a solid hour on that difficult spreadsheet, put some distance between yourself and the screen. Your brain does not need random, non-essential data to distract it from the business at hand. And your connections can wait.

It may sound counterintuitive, but taking regular, short breaks—even if you are not hungry, thirsty, or annoyed—increases your productivity over chaining yourself to the desk. In fact, a change of scenery is often exactly what your brain needs to keep going or sort out a thorny problem. Get up, stretch, step outside, take some deep breaths, soak in a few minutes of sunshine, smell a flower, or go for a walk. Eat a healthy snack or make a cup of tea.

Then go back to finish what you started. Give yourself a break, and you'll be able to give your best.

Digital Breaks, Digital Sabbaths, Digital Detoxes

If you are intentional, morning PRESENT time can teach you how to put down your devices for longer periods of time. Even so, while many of us know the importance of longer disconnections—for a full day, a weekend, a real vacation—most of us don't do it. Pushing pause just on social media, only one facet of our always-on age, has so far been too big a challenge for a majority of people: 60% admit they've *never* taken a break. That's two out of three people checking Facebook, Twitter, Tumblr, Instagram, or all of the above every single day into infinity.

The consequences are no small thing. Fifteen years ago, MIT professor Sherry Turkle extolled the many blessings connectedness would bring us, extending our real-world relationships across time and space and changing for the better how we would connect and stay connected with others. But after a decade and a half studying how people use their connected devices, Professor Turkle has done a virtual 180. In her book

Alone Together: Why We Expect More from Technology and Less from Each Other, she presents her findings that dissatisfaction and alienation have risen in tandem with our adoption of social media.[18] It is possible, of course, to nurture relationships online that go beyond the illusion of companionship to real intimacy and friendship. Real intimacy and friendships come by learning relational skills when navigating everyday, face-to-face connections with family and friends. But the more time we spend online, the less time we spend honing the skills we need to create meaningful relationships in both on- and off-line spaces.

But on top of that, because online relationships are lived at arm's length, they can distort our perception of ourselves and others.

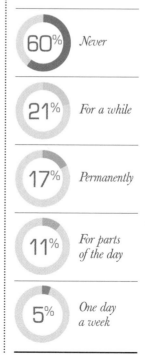

DIGITAL DETOX

When asked if they take regular breaks from social media, a striking majority of adults say they never unplug.

60% *Never*

21% *For a while*

17% *Permanently*

11% *For parts of the day*

5% *One day a week*

Shauna Niequist wrote a piece for *RELEVANT* magazine that resonated deeply with me. She says:

> I keep having the same conversation over and over ... It starts like this: "I gave up Facebook for Lent, and I realized I'm a lot happier without it." Or like this: "Pinterest makes me hate my house." Or like this: "I stopped following a friend on Instagram, and now that I don't see nonstop snapshots of her perfect life, I like her better."[19]

Many of the respondents to the FRAMES survey might identify with these sentiments. When we relate primarily online, we tend to see everyone else's life as better than ours and often come away feeling bad about ourselves. Viewed through the distorting prism of social media, our friends appear more creative, successful, wealthy, and attractive than we believe ourselves to be. Of course, when we feel inferior or insecure, we are even less likely to extend ourselves with the kind of vulnerability that real and meaningful relationships demand. And thus the downward spiral continues.

Taking intentional time out from our connected lives, however, helps us remove our pixel-colored glasses and regain a perspective closer to reality. Yet the trend of a digital Sabbath has yet to catch on. Although 11% of respondents claim that they set aside time each day to break from social media, just 5% takes a regular day-long break each week.

Matthew Sleeth's popular book *24/6: A Prescription for a Healthier, Happier Life* argues that Sabbath practice is more essential than ever for our modern lives.

Sadly, however, though many of us agree in principle to "Remember the Sabbath day by keeping it holy" (Exodus 20:8), most of us have no idea how to practice a day of intentional rest in a 24/7, always-on world. Sleeth explains Sabbath this way:

> Just as the Hebrews were slaves in Egypt, we have become slaves to technology. Our technological tools allow 24-hour productivity and connectivity, give us more control, and subtly enslave us to busyness itself. Sabbath is about restraint, about intentionally not doing everything all the time just because we can. Setting aside a day of rest helps us reconnect with our Creator and find the peace of God that passes all understanding. The Sabbath is about letting go of the controls one day a week and letting God be God.[20]

If one day a week sounds like an eternity, it's time to go cold turkey and plan a digital detox. Even for people who keep a consistent digital Sabbath, a longer period of complete disconnection can be refreshing and perspective-enhancing. A 2013 *Fast Company* feature chronicled the off-line experience of the "world's most connected man." The headline says it all: "#UNPLUG: Baratunde Thurston Left the Internet for 25 Days, and You Should, Too."[21]

As you might imagine, the rules of a digital detox can vary. In Thurston's plan, text messages and phone calls were allowed. For Susan Maushart, author of *The Winter of Our Disconnect: How Three Totally Wired Teenagers (and a Mother Who Slept with Her iPhone) Pulled the Plug on Their Technology and Lived to Tell the*

On a regular basis I ...

54%
1 / *Relax*

45%
2 / *Exercise*

44%
3 / *Enjoy a hobby*

42%
4 / *Spend time with friends*

39%
5 / *Say "no" to more activities*

37%
6 / *Pray or meditate*

35%
7 / *Set goals*

Tale, texting was off the table. Some digital detox devotees allow a daily email check to ensure things haven't gotten out of hand. The rules are up to you, but the goal is simply this: get your mind and body away from the screen.

The effects can be astounding. Maushart's book reveals that one result of her six-month experiment to take herself and her teenage children entirely off-line was a dramatic difference in her kids' sleep patterns.[22] Without constantly chiming smartphones, the family was able to pay back a sleep debt they had been carrying for years. In 2012, when I took twelve days off-line, the immediate result was exactly what I hoped for: when I returned to the Internet, I felt excited to reconnect and invigorated to tackle the projects ahead.

A few key things can predict your ability to disconnect well. As I found, the amount of planning was directly correlated with how free I felt to proceed. By ensuring I had simple email auto-responses set up on all my accounts, explaining that I would be unavailable and providing direction to folks looking for answers in my absence, I felt free not to respond to email. I also scheduled blog posts and social media messages ahead of time to post during my break so I would still have an online presence while I was away. Finally, I included my phone number on my email auto responses, letting people know they could get in touch in case of emergency. Doing so meant that more than one person texted with an issue that wasn't particularly urgent, but knowing my bases were covered gave me the mental freedom to truly disconnect.

Maybe pulling away entirely from the Internet — for one day or twenty-five — seems completely unfeasible, perhaps because of professional demands. But I urge you to consider it. Yes, there are some people for whom complete disconnection is genuinely difficult (an on-call doctor, for instance) and occasions when going dark is not a good idea (when you're on deadline or when your website gets a link on the CNN.com home page). But chances are, you will have a window in the next six months during which you can realistically take an extended vacation from the Internet. If you take it, I can come *this* close to guaranteeing you will return to the online world with fresh perspective and a refreshed spirit.

First Things First

We all want to live whole and fulfilled lives, full of meaning and promise that reflect our passions and embody our values. Unfortunately, many of us spend our days not living the life we dream of. Instead, we just try to keep our head above water, flailing in a sea of text message notifications, banner ads, Facebook likes, and forwarded bogus emails from relatives who don't know how to use Snopes.com. We don't live into our goals or priorities, but rather react, react, react to the next demand and the next and the next.

You can turn the tide, starting with your mornings. Begin with the PRESENT Principle—*pray, read, express, schedule, exercise, nourish, track*—and prioritize your well-being each day. Take a weekly digital Sabbath to rest in mind and spirit, letting God be God while you take a break. On a quarterly or semiannual basis, go dark for a few days, a week, or longer to regain your perspective on yourself, on your use of technology, and on the things that are of importance for your life, family, and purpose.

When things go wrong, get back on course quickly and with kindness to yourself. If it's 11:30 on Monday morning and you're still getting a BuzzFeed fix, with nary a task completed since Friday, step away from the screen. Don't beat yourself up; just take a few minutes to redirect your focus and willpower toward your priorities.

Our on-demand, all-access, always-on age is, let's face it, an exciting time to be alive. The tools at our disposal can be immeasurable blessings—but only as long as we use them wisely with thoughtful reflection and clear intentions. When reflection and intentionality start to sound strange and exotic, you can bet the black hole of greater and greater expectations is exerting its gravitational pull and you're in danger of falling in. One simple act can set you free: *disconnect*.

Sometimes.

Your life will thank you. ◆

GREATER EXPECTATIONS

Succeed (and Stay Sane) in an On-Demand,
All-Access, Always-On Age

RE/FRAME

BY DIANE PADDISON

Imagine sitting down for one of those extremely important work meetings that keep you up the night before as you mentally go over—again and again—your presentation. Your boss is there. Your CEO is there. All eyes are on you. Then, just as things are getting started, your cell phone rings—and it's your teenage daughter.

What do you do?

I take the call—every time—because my daughter knows not to call unless her need is truly urgent. And because my coworkers and superiors know that, while I'm fully committed to my job, my family ultimately comes first. Furthermore, I've built up a relationship of trust at work, establishing myself as someone who works hard, produces results, and who exercises good judgment.

I began putting this work ethic into practice when I was five years old, operating the cash register at my family's orchard and fruit stand outside of Harrisburg, Oregon. And I developed them even more as an executive in two Fortune 500 companies, who went on to sit on multiple corporate boards, launch a nonprofit ministry, and raise a family of my own. It certainly hasn't all been easy, but if there's anything that's helped me along the way, it's learning to create and keep up healthy boundaries.

When you're in that important meeting and your phone rings with an urgent personal need, you should take the call too, but not before you've laid some important groundwork.

Seek out the right work environment

The best way to maintain healthy boundaries is to work for a company that respects them. Pay attention to the cues while you're interviewing. Note how much travel will be required of you. Listen carefully to how people talk about their work and what it demands of them. It's a bad sign if you hear employees say things like, "You're gonna love it here, but you might want to keep a sleeping bag under your desk."

Is it harder to find a family-friendly job? Maybe so, and in a difficult job market or if you are the sole breadwinner for your family, holding firmly to those priorities may not be in your best interests. If you need to take a job that will infringe on your preferred personal and family time, however, be up front with your children and let them know they will have to make some sacrifices until you can find a better job. Do keep looking, though, because eventually the clash between your values and your work will take its toll.

Work with integrity

I've always felt if I'm going to establish boundaries between my work and my faith and my family, I need to make sure that when I am at work, I give 100%. Part of that comes from growing up on a farm, where I never wanted anyone to think the boss's daughter got off easier than anyone else. But doing your best is also part of honoring God's calling to work.

It's been my experience that people at work are much more likely to respect and support my boundaries when they have already seen me work hard to get the job done.

Communicate well and often

Boundaries are much more effective when the people around you know and understand them. My loved ones know they can count on me to be home every night by six for dinner. They know they can call me anytime while I'm at work if they have an urgent need. All these factors communicate to them that as much as I am committed to my job, my family comes first.

Likewise, at work I let my team know that I will be leaving in time to make it home for dinner, but that I will be available (and working as needed) for a few hours after the kids go to bed.

Of course, life has a way of getting messy, and there will be times when you have to miss dinner with your family or arrive at work late. Boundaries can flex when needed; the key is to make sure those occasions are few and far between and that you communicate clearly in both directions.

Manage your commitments

As you probably already know, your career alone can consume you. Add in family responsibilities, further education, kids' activities, and church or charitable commitments, and you'll be exhausted by looking at your calendar before the week has even begun.

If you say yes to everything, you will get burned out and you won't be putting in your best efforts anywhere.

To make your commitments count, you must learn to say no to a lot of worthy causes and endeavors and instead pick a few key areas of focus that provide the most value. Remember that there is a time and a season for everything (see Ecclesiastes 3:1–11).

Be a good steward of yourself

Your health and sanity are resources God has given you, and they should be stewarded accordingly. Maintaining balance between work, family, and faith requires energy, creativity, flexibility, and a healthy dose of optimism. A half-hearted or crippled effort simply won't do. That's why it's crucial to take good care of yourself. You must guard your physical, emotional, mental, and spiritual health if you want to succeed. Exercise regularly, eat well, and set aside time for your own enjoyment and relaxation.

A little investment in "you" will yield huge dividends. You'll have more energy, a clearer head, and the emotional capacity needed to balance all that life throws at you. There will be days when you look at your planner and think, "I don't possibly have time today to eat, sleep, and rest well!" But here's the thing about boundaries: when you set them in place, your work will be better for it. ◆

....

Diane Paddison is the founder of 4word (4wordwomen.org), a nonprofit organization seeking to lead, connect, and support professional Christian women to reach their God-given potential, and the author of *Work, Love, Pray*, from which this article is adapted. She is the chief strategy officer of Cassidy Turley and former two-time global executive team member of two Fortune 500 Companies, CBRE and ProLogis. She serves on the Salvation Army's National Advisory Board and the board of Harvard Business School's Christian Fellowship Alumni Association.

AFTER YOU READ

- When you think about implementing the PRESENT Principle in your life, which of the steps most excites or intrigues you? Which step seems most difficult to adopt? Why?

- Would you describe yourself as burned out and/ or behind? If you analyze your current habits and practices, what do you think is contributing to those feelings? How might incorporating some of the PRESENT practices or implementing some scheduling and prioritizing help you?

- In what ways is your perspective on yourself and others distorted by social media? How might taking intentional time away help you see more clearly?

- Do you feel an element of "need" when it comes to online engagement? Where do you think that need comes from?

- How is your spiritual life affected by your level of connectedness? How does being "always on" enhance or hinder your pursuit of God?

- What day of the week could work for you as a regular digital Sabbath? What preparations or plans do you need to make so you can feel free to disconnect?

- Do you make regular time to engage with your kids, significant other, friends, or close family members without your devices? What are some off-line activities you can do together to nurture your relationship?

ABOUT THE RESEARCH

FRAMES started with the idea that people need simple, clear ideas to live more meaningful lives in the midst of increasingly complex times. To help make sense of culture, each FRAME includes major public opinion studies conducted by Barna Group.

If you're into the details, the research behind the *Greater Expectations* FRAME included 1,086 surveys conducted among a representative sample of adults over the age of 18 living in the United States. The survey was conducted from May 10, 2013, through May 20, 2013. An additional poll included 1,000 surveys conducted among a representative sample of adults over the age of 18 living in the United States and included an oversample of 494 interviews completed by 18- to 29-year-olds. This survey was conducted from June 25, 2013, through July 1, 2013. The sampling error for both surveys is plus or minus 3 percentage points, at the 95% confidence level.

If you're really into the research details, find more at www.barnaframes.com.

ABOUT BARNA GROUP

In its thirty-year history, Barna Group has conducted more than one million interviews over the course of hundreds of studies and has become a go-to source for insights about faith and culture. Currently led by David Kinnaman, Barna Group's vision is to provide people with credible knowledge and clear thinking, enabling them to navigate a complex and changing culture. The company was started by George and Nancy Barna in 1984.

Barna Group has worked with thousands of businesses, nonprofit organizations, and churches across the country, including many Protestant and Catholic congregations and denominations. Some of its clients have included the American Bible Society, CARE, Compassion, Easter Seals, Habitat for Humanity, NBC Universal, the Salvation Army, Walden Media, the ONE Campaign, SONY, Thrivent, US AID, and World Vision.

The firm's studies are frequently used in sermons and talks. And its public opinion research is often quoted in major media outlets, such as *CNN, USA Today*, the *Wall Street Journal*, Fox News, *Chicago Tribune*, the *Huffington Post,* the *New York Times*, *Dallas Morning News*, and the *Los Angeles Times*.

Learn more about Barna Group at www.barna.org.

THANKS

Even small books take enormous effort.

First, thanks go to Claire Diaz-Ortiz for her insightful, swift, and good work on this FRAME—offering her lessons learned (some the hard way) and her always practical wisdom to create what we pray is a prophetic call to live a different kind of life within the greater and greater expectations of the twenty-first century.

We are also incredibly grateful for the contribution of Diane Paddison, who has been cultivating these healthy habits in a culture of "greater expectations" for many years now.

Next, Barna Group gratefully acknowledges the efforts of the team at HarperCollins Christian Publishing, especially Chip Brown and Melinda Bouma for catching the vision from the get-go. Others at HarperCollins who have made huge contributions include Jennifer Keller, Kate Mulvaney, Mark Sheeres, and Shari Vanden Berg.

The FRAMES team at Barna Group consists of Elaina Buffon, Bill Denzel, Traci Hochmuth, Pam Jacob, Clint Jenkin, Robert Jewe, David Kinnaman, Jill Kinnaman, Elaine Klautzsch, Stephanie Smith, and Roxanne Stone. Bill and Stephanie consistently made magic out of thin air. Clint and Traci brought the research to life—along with thoughtful analysis from Ken Chitwood. And Roxanne deserves massive credit as a shaping force on FRAMES. Amy Duty did heroic work on FRAMES designs, from cover to infographics.

Finally, others who have had a huge role in bringing FRAMES to life include Brad Abare, Justin Bell, Jean Bloom, Patrick Dodd, Grant England, Esther Fedorkevich, Josh Franer, Jane Haradine, Aly Hawkins, Kelly Hughes, Steve McBeth, Geof Morin, Jesse Oxford, Beth Shagene, and Santino Stoner.

Many thanks!

NOTES

1. "Deputy UN Chief Calls for Urgent Action to Tackle Global Sanitation Crisis," UN News Centre (March 21, 2013): http://www.un.org/apps/news/story.asp?NewsID=44452&Cr=sanitation&Cr1=#.Ujcu-Lwd4mR.

2. "Social Media Statistics and Facts 2012," *GO-Globe* (October 30, 2012): http://www.go-globe.com/blog/social-media-facts/.

3. Ronald Pies, MD, "Should DSM-V Designate 'Internet Addiction' a Mental Disorder?" *Psychiatry MMC* (February 6, 2009): http://www.ncbi.nlm.nih.gov/pmc/articles/PMC2719452/.

4. "Americans Just Want a Good Night of Sleep," Barna Group (October 13, 2006): https://www.barna.org/barna-update/culture/145-americans-just-want-a-good-night-of-sleep.

5. Laura Hudson, "Q&A: Claire Diaz-Ortiz, the Woman Who Got the Pope on Twitter," *Wired* (December 17, 2012): http://www.wired.com/underwire/2012/12/pope-twitter-interview/.

6. Patrick Klingaman, *Finding Rest When the Work Is Never Done* (Colorado Springs, CO: David C. Cook, 2002), 9.

7. Elizabeth Cohen, "Do You Obsessively Check Your Smartphone?" *CNN Health* (July 28, 2011): http://www.cnn.com/2011/HEALTH/07/28/ep.smartphone.obsessed.cohen/index.html.

8. Roy F. Baumeister and John Tierney, *Willpower: Rediscovering the Greatest Human Strength* (New York: Penguin Press, 2011), 20–39.

9. James W. Pennebaker, *Writing to Heal: A Guided Journal for Recovering from Trauma and Emotional Upheaval* (Oakland, CA: New Harbinger Publications, 2004), 4–6.

10. For a terrific example of a mind map, see "The 100 Most Creative People in Business 2012: Greg Gunn," *Fast Company* (May, 2012): http://www.fastcompany.com/most-creative -people/2012/greg-gunn.

11. Eviatar Zerubavel, *The Clockwork Muse: A Practical Guide to Writing Theses, Dissertations, and Books* (Cambridge, MA: Harvard University Press, 1999).

12. Amy Lynn Andrews, *Tell Your Time: How to Manage Your Schedule So You Can Live Free* (Amy Lynn Andrews e-book ed., 2011).

13. "On the Move," *The Simple Mom Podcast*, Episode 10 (November 2, 2011): http://homefries.com/show/the-simple-mom -podcast/the-simple-mom-podcast-episode-10-on-the-move/.

14. Gretchen Rubin, *The Happiness Project: Or, Why I Spent a Year Trying to Sing in the Morning, Clean My Closets, Fight Right, Read Aristotle, and Generally Have More Fun* (New York: Harper Paperbacks, reprint ed., 2011).

15. Dean Fleischer-Camp and Jenny Slate, "Marcel the Shell with Shoes On, Two," YouTube (November 4, 2011): http://www .youtube.com/watch?v=Ta9K22D0o5Q.

16. My Scan-to-Plan method draws on ideas from two of my favorite scheduling books: *Getting Things Done: The Art of Stress-Free Productivity* by David Allen (New York: Penguin Books, 2002) and *The Power of Full Engagement: Managing Energy, Not Time, Is the Key to High Performance and Personal Renewal* by Jim Loehr and Tony Schwartz (New York: Free Press, 2005).

17. Brian Tracy, *Eat That Frog! Get More of the Important Things Done Today* (London, UK: Hodder Paperback, 2013).

18. Sherry Turkle, *Alone Together: Why We Expect More from Technology and Less from Each Other* (New York: Basic Books, 2012).

19. Shauna Niequist, "Instagram's Envy Effect," *RELEVANT* (April 4, 2013): http://www.relevantmagazine.com/culture/tech/stop-instagramming-your-perfect-life.

20. Matthew Sleeth, *24/6: A Prescription for a Healthier, Happier Life* (Carol Stream, IL: Tyndale, 2012): http://matthewsleethmd.com/246-a-prescription-for-a-healthier-happier-life/.

21. Baratunde Thurston, "#UNPLUG: Baratunde Thurston Left the Internet for 25 Days, and You Should, Too," *Fast Company* (June 17, 2013): http://www.fastcompany.com/3012521/unplug/baratunde-thurston-leaves-the-internet.

22. Susan Maushart, *The Winter of Our Disconnect: How Three Totally Wired Teenagers (and a Mother Who Slept with Her iPhone) Pulled the Plug on Their Technology and Lived to Tell the Tale* (Los Angeles: Tarcher, reprint ed., 2011), 232–241.

Share Your Thoughts

With the Author: Your comments will be forwarded to the author when you send them to *zauthor@zondervan.com*.

With Zondervan: Submit your review of this book by writing to *zreview@zondervan.com*.

Free Online Resources at
www.zondervan.com

Daily Bible Verses and Devotions: Enrich your life with daily Bible verses or devotions that help you start every morning focused on God. Visit www.zondervan.com/newsletters.

Free Email Publications: Sign up for newsletters on Christian living, academic resources, church ministry, fiction, children's resources, and more. Visit www.zondervan.com/newsletters.

Zondervan Bible Search: Find and compare Bible passages in a variety of translations at www.zondervanbiblesearch.com.

Other Benefits: Register to receive online benefits like coupons and special offers, or to participate in research.